Voices From The Past ✶ ✶ ✶ ✶ ✶ ✶ ✶ ✶ ✶ ✶

PERSIAN GULF WAR

KATHLYN GAY   MARTIN GAY

Twenty-First Century Books
A Division of Henry Holt and Company
New York

Twenty-First Century Books
A Division of Henry Holt and Company, Inc.
115 West 18th Street
New York, NY 10011

Henry Holt® and colophon are trademarks of
Henry Holt and Company, Inc.
Publishers since 1866

Published in Canada by Fitzhenry & Whiteside Ltd.
195 Allstate Parkway, Markham, Ontario L3R 4T8

Library of Congress Cataloging-in-Publication Data
Gay, Kathlyn.
Persian Gulf War / Kathlyn Gay and Martin Gay.—1st ed.
p.   cm.—(Voices from the past)
Includes bibliographical references (p.   ) and index.
Summary: Describes the circumstances leading up to Iran's
invasion of Kuwait and the political and military events of the
Persian Gulf War, using quotes from people directly involved.
1. Persian Gulf War, 1991—Juvenile literature. [1. Persian Gulf War, 1991.]
I .Gay, Martin, 1950–   . II. Title. III Series:
Gay, Kathlyn. Voices from the past.
DS79.723.G39   1996
956.7044'2—dc20   96-15579
                                                                                      CIP
                                                                                      AC

ISBN 0-8050-4102-8
First Edition—1996

Printed in the United States of America
All first editions are printed on acid-free paper. ∞
1 3 5 7 9 10 8 6 4 2

Cover design by Karen Quigley
Interior design by Kelly Soong

Cover: *Steel Rain:The Army National Guard in Desert Storm* by Mort Künstler
Courtesy of National Guard Heritage Series, Dept. of the Army,
National Guard Bureau, Washington, D.C.

Photo credits
p. 6: van der Stockt/Gamma Liaison; pp. 11, 16, 33: UPI/Corbis-Bettmann; p. 24:
Consolidated News Pictures/Archive Photos; p. 25: Corbis-Bettmann; pp. 26, 42:
Department of Defense; p. 30: Paul Miller/Black Star; p. 35: Photri, Inc.; p. 39:
Jacqueline Artz/Black Star; p. 47: AP/Wide World Photos; p. 49: Peter Turnley/
Black Star; p. 53: Hires/Merillon/Gamma Liaison.

Contents

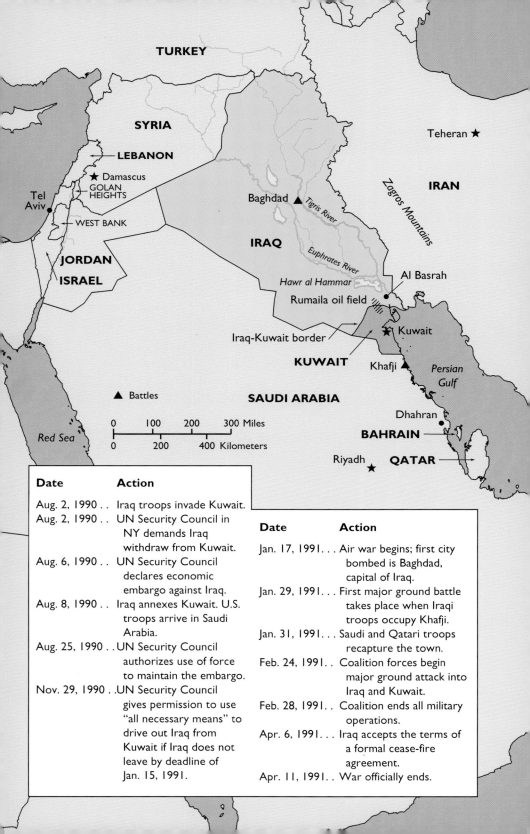

TURKEY

SYRIA

LEBANON

★ Damascus
GOLAN
HEIGHTS

Tel
Aviv

WEST BANK

JORDAN

ISRAEL

IRAQ

Baghdad ▲ Tigris River

Euphrates River

Hawr al Hammar

Rumaila oil field

Iraq-Kuwait border

KUWAIT

Teheran ★

IRAN

Zagros Mountains

Al Basrah

★ Kuwait

Khafji ▲ Persian
Gulf

▲ Battles

SAUDI ARABIA

Dhahran

0   100   200   300 Miles

BAHRAIN

Red Sea

0   200   400 Kilometers

Riyadh
★   QATAR

Date	Action
Aug. 2, 1990 . .	Iraq troops invade Kuwait.
Aug. 2, 1990 . .	UN Security Council in NY demands Iraq withdraw from Kuwait.
Aug. 6, 1990 . .	UN Security Council declares economic embargo against Iraq.
Aug. 8, 1990 . .	Iraq annexes Kuwait. U.S. troops arrive in Saudi Arabia.
Aug. 25, 1990 . .	UN Security Council authorizes use of force to maintain the embargo.
Nov. 29, 1990 . .	UN Security Council gives permission to use "all necessary means" to drive out Iraq from Kuwait if Iraq does not leave by deadline of Jan. 15, 1991.

Date	Action
Jan. 17, 1991 . . .	Air war begins; first city bombed is Baghdad, capital of Iraq.
Jan. 29, 1991 . . .	First major ground battle takes place when Iraqi troops occupy Khafji.
Jan. 31, 1991 . . .	Saudi and Qatari troops recapture the town.
Feb. 24, 1991 . .	Coalition forces begin major ground attack into Iraq and Kuwait.
Feb. 28, 1991 . .	Coalition ends all military operations.
Apr. 6, 1991 . . .	Iraq accepts the terms of a formal cease-fire agreement.
Apr. 11, 1991 . .	War officially ends.

One

✦

WAR! LIVE ON TV

$\mathcal{A}$ few minutes after 6:30 P.M. on January 16, 1991, eastern standard time, Cable News Network (CNN) came on the air with a special report from the ancient city of Baghdad in Iraq, where it was already the next day, January 17. Broadcasting live from their room in the Al Rashid Hotel, Peter Arnett, Bernard Shaw, and John Holliman became the eyes and ears of the world.

The men had been awakened just after 2:30 A.M. Baghdad time by the loud concussion of explosions and the incessant rat-a-tat-tat of antiaircraft weapons. Tracings of red and white light brightened the sky over the capital city. To the reporters, it looked like this was the night they had been waiting for. As they reported in their telecast:

> **Shaw:** Something is happening outside. . . . The skies over Baghdad have been illuminated. We're seeing bright flashes going off all over the sky. Peter . . .
>
> **Arnett:** Now the sirens are sounding for the first time.
>
> **Holliman:** Whoa! Holy Cow! That was a large airburst that we saw, filling the sky . . .
>
> **Arnett:** And I think, John, that airburst took out the telecommunications . . .

Holliman: Now you may see the bombs now, if you're still with us, you can hear the bombs now . . .

Shaw: Just one comment . . . clearly I've never been there, but this feels like we're in the center of hell.[1]

This broadcast was just one of many that CNN reporters would make from "behind the lines" in the enemy camp. Other stations devoted a great deal of their airtime to coverage of the war, but American and international television viewers came to rely on the reports from CNN. In a few short days, the network became the number one source for news around the world, as they transformed the fighting over the skies of Iraq into the first "Live TV War" in history.

Allied night bombing of Baghdad, January 17, 1991

"FIREWORKS" OVER BAGHDAD

Few who saw the first night's TV broadcast viewed from the window of the Al Rashid will ever forget it. And those who were on the scene experienced what seemed to be an unreal event. Michael Kelly, a freelance reporter in Baghdad for the print media, wrote his vivid recollection of that early morning attack:

> You would have to be blind not to be transfixed. The city was blacked out, and the sky above it was a deep purple, with the silhouettes of the taller buildings just visible as dark-gray edges. Against this the tracer rounds made lines of incandescent beauty, lovely arcing curves and slow S's and parabolas of light. . . .
>
> The guns made a great mess of sound that worked itself out, after a minute or so, into an almost symphonic order, the big 57-millimeters booming with deep bass thuds against a chattering of lesser artillery. I thought then that the large sounds were bombs, but I read later that this was not so.[2]

Kelly and Americans watching TV safely in their homes saw only the results of the defensive barrage put up by the Iraqi armed forces. Although Iraqi airspace had been violated, the first attack, led by the United States, was occurring miles away from the capital city on the southwestern border of Iraq, where destruction of part of the forward surveillance network was taking place.

"It was ten seconds before 2:38 in the black, moonless morning," wrote Lieutenant General Edward Flanagan Jr. in his insider's account of the history of the 101st Aviation Brigade. He reported that

> Task Force Normandy's two teams of four AH-64 Apache helicopter crews hovered at fifty feet over their targets 50

miles inside Iraq. On their forward-looking infrared screens (FLIRS), the pilots saw them—two Iraqi radar sites that were linked to four Iraqi fighter bases and the Intelligence Operations Center in Baghdad. . . .

Lt. Tom Drew was in charge of this important mission that had been designed to disrupt the "Command and Control" network for the Iraq air defense system. "Party in ten," he said, breaking radio silence for the first time on the mission. Ten seconds later, the Apaches launched a salvo of laser-guided Hellfire missiles. Desert Storm had begun.[3]

OPERATION DESERT STORM

Around 2:45 A.M., the attack known as Operation Desert Storm was expanded to targets in and around Baghdad. U.S. F-117 Stealth fighter planes dropped their bombs on the telephone exchange, the communications centers, and many of Iraq's military headquarters. Within a few hours, major facilities that controlled the air defenses of Iraq were almost completely destroyed. Those air defenses had been designed to direct countermeasures against invading armies and attacking planes, but with their loss, Iraqi dictator Saddam Hussein's grand plan to make himself the dominant power in the modern Arab world was in jeopardy. Hussein would soon discover that his scheme would be literally blown to bits by a multinational force that launched what is known as the Persian Gulf War, or simply the Gulf War.

Hussein had initiated the conflict months before when he invaded the small neighboring kingdom of Kuwait. His motives have been the subject of numerous essays, books, and TV programs. Besides Hussein's desire for power, the reasons for the war also stem from ancient rivalries and territorial disputes along the Persian Gulf (once called the Arabian Gulf), where much of the world's oil is produced.

Two

★

THE RISE OF SADDAM HUSSEIN

Saddam means "one who confronts," a fitting name for the man who rules the people of Iraq. Saddam Hussein was raised in a world dominated by foreigners who had controlled the land of his birth for many years. By the time he took the reigns of government, Hussein was more than ready to confront those whom he blamed for the misuse of his country's people and resources. Some political analysts have also suggested that he saw himself as heir to the great Nebuchadnezzar, emperor of the ancient Babylonian Empire that flourished in Iraq about 600 B.C. Hussein was driven, they say, to see his people reclaim their birthright in the land known as the "cradle of civilization."

The area occupied by Iraq, Iran, Kuwait, Syria, Lebanon, and Israel is defined as the Middle East, or Mideast. (Many scholars include Libya, Egypt, and other surrounding nations as part of the Mideast as well.) According to legend, this is where the great civilizations of the Western world first developed in the land between the Tigris and Euphrates Rivers: the biblical Garden of Eden.

CENTURIES OF STRIFE

For centuries, this ancient land has also been the site of upheaval because of its strategic location between Africa,

Europe, and Asia. Many nations wanted to control the area in order to make a profit on the great trade routes that crossed the desert. As a result, powerful foreign armies have taken turns occupying this land where traditional Muslim nomadic tribes have lived simple lives for many generations.

In the nineteenth century, Turkey was the center of the well-established Ottoman Empire that considered much of the Middle East its own. Their strong military presence kept the Arab tribes divided and at bay until World War I. Then, as an ally of Germany, the Turkish Empire fought the French and British to retain control of its colonized land to the south. The British armies had excellent success in uniting the Arab tribes for the first time, creating the basis for a revolutionary movement that was able to overthrow the Ottomans.

At the end of World War I, the British and the French refused to leave the region, even though Great Britain had promised the Arabs that they could build their own nations in exchange for supporting the Allies. The Europeans declared that they would decide when the tribes could have their independence. While the French maintained control of the land where Syria and Lebanon are today, Britain administered the areas of Jordan, Palestine, and Iraq, where the British controlled major oil production facilities.

As angry as they were at this betrayal of trust, the Arabs were still too weak to throw off the combined might of the new masters. Rubbing more salt into the wounds of these Islamic tribes, the British also supported the notion that Jews, another religious group with roots in the Middle East, had the right to establish their own separate state in the region. It appeared that the Jewish minority was given preference over the Muslim majority already well established in the land known as Palestine, the place Britain now designated as a Jewish homeland. The intense resentment created by

During the time of British control, there were many
confrontations between British soldiers and Arabs.

the actions of the French and especially the British would
fester for decades.

LINES IN THE SAND

Resentment increased in 1922 when British leaders decided
to redraw the boundaries between Iraq and the emirate of
Kuwait, ignoring ancient tribal claims and traditional trade
routes. The kingdom of Kuwait had been established early in

the eighteenth century on land that was once considered part of Iraq (Babylon). It became a British protectorate in 1899 when the emir (king) signed an agreement to be represented by Britain in all foreign affairs. Emir Mubarak al-Sabah was one of a long line of Kuwait rulers chosen from within the royal Sabah family, who are still in power today.

With the new boundaries, Iraq obtained a little more mainland area, but Kuwait was given possession of two key islands on the Persian Gulf. As a result, Iraq was cut off from this body of water, important for the export of its wealth-producing oil from the Rumaila (Rumaylah) oil field on the Kuwait-Iraq border. Both countries pump this valuable resource from this reserve.

By cutting off Iraq, the British were able to maintain their control of the Gulf. As British diplomat Anthony Parsons acknowledged years later: "We protected our strategic interests rather successfully, but in doing so we didn't worry too much about the people living there. We created a situation where people felt they had been wronged."[1]

During the time the British dominated affairs in both Iraq and Kuwait, they allowed King Feisal I to rule Iraq under their authority from 1921 until its independence in 1932. Feisal was content to give Britain great influence over his country's affairs. In 1939, Feisal's grandson, Feisal II, assumed the throne, but in 1958 he was gunned down in a coup d'état (violent overthrow) that began a series of successive revolts. As a result, no real leadership came to power until the 1970s.

During this period of political strife in Iraq, the British granted Kuwait its independence in 1961 and withdrew its protection of the emirate. Immediately thereafter the Iraqis claimed Kuwait as part of their ancestral home. To prevent an Iraqi takeover, the British quickly sent troops to occupy defensive positions throughout the kingdom.

Once again in 1973, the Iraqis pressed their claims. This time, the regime in power, the brutal and militaristic Ba'ath Socialist Party, ordered troops to invade a coastal section of Kuwait. Under pressure from the international community, the Iraqi forces left. But six years later, Saddam Hussein had risen from the ranks to lead the Ba'athists.

FIRST CONFRONTATIONS

Saddam Hussein joined the Ba'ath Party in the 1950s, and early on he stood out among the membership. In 1958, he was known to have killed his brother-in-law, a supporter of the very popular General Abdul Qassim, who had taken over the government. The following year, when the Ba'athists initially attempted to seize power, Hussein was part of a failed attempt to assassinate Qassim. When the Ba'athists finally did murder Qassim in February 1963, establishing themselves as the government of Iraq, Hussein was given the responsibility of interrogator and torturer at the main political detention facility.

"My arms and legs were bound by rope," remembers an Iraqi prisoner who was personally tortured by Hussein for plotting against the Ba'aths. "I was hung on the rope to a hook on the ceiling and I was repeatedly beaten with rubber hoses filled with stones."[2]

Another unfortunate prisoner, journalist Sami Fraj Ali, reported that Hussein wasn't always the one wielding the hose. "He was the man who gave the orders. He had the authority, with one word, to decide if you stayed alive or died. I was brought into a big room with Saddam and about twelve people who worked for him. By the time he interrogated me, I had already been beaten by others. . . . He said to me: 'This time we scared you. But next time you will not survive. We will hang you.' "[3]

Hussein was adept at creating a secret police organization that gave him the basis for real power within the Ba'ath Party, and he had cultivated the reputation of one who should be feared. By the late 1970s he was taking over more and more of the daily presidential duties in his role as "Mr. Deputy," a title he insisted upon as the second in command of the Iraqi government. On July 16, 1979, Ahmad Hasan al-Bakr either resigned from the presidency or was bullied out of the office by the "one who confronts." The next day Saddam Hussein became president.

Three

*K*ING OF THE HILL

September 22, 1980, was the day Saddam Hussein decided to stride onto the world's stage by attacking his Muslim-fundamentalist neighbor, Iran. His excuse? Iraq had a right to control the Shatt-al-Arab waterway that divided the two nations. However, Hussein was more likely acting out of his fear of the Ayatollah Ruhollah Khomeini, an Iranian religious leader. The Ayatollah had come to power in February 1979, when an Islamic revolution swept the government of Muhammad Reza Shah Pahlavi out of office and out of Iran.

Khomeini was the acknowledged world leader of the Shiite sect of Muslim Arabs. Iran is 93 percent Shiite, and Iraq had a substantial (15 percent) Shiite minority living within its borders. Thus, Hussein feared that the Ayatollah would use this sect to export his fundamentalist revolution to Iraq, a country with which Iran had had many grievances in the past.

Striking first to establish his supremacy in the Middle East, Hussein's troops quickly occupied portions of Iran. His ground forces were greatly outnumbered by the Iranian army, which sent numerous "human wave" attacks against Iraqi positions.

By June 1982, the Iraqis were driven out of Iran, but their superior air power was able to keep the fight going. It

Saddam Hussein addressing his nation in
late September 1980 after Iraq had attacked Iran

lasted for another six years, spreading to the Persian Gulf, where both nations fired upon ships and aircraft from neutral countries. Eventually, after an estimated one million people had lost their lives, a cease-fire was negotiated by the United Nations.

EFFECTS OF THE LONG WAR

No territory changed hands in the Iran-Iraq War, but Saddam Hussein gained a reputation as a ruthless and inhuman aggressor. News reports showed that he had used chemical weapon bombs (poison gas) on his own people. Iraqi Kurds, an ethnic minority that supported Iran during the fighting, paid the ultimate price for their disloyalty—thousands were killed or forced to flee the country.

The great oil wealth of Iraq had allowed Hussein to build his country into a model of economic progress for the area, but the strain of maintaining a huge army in the field for such a long period had cost him much. Because of the war, Hussein had negotiated loans from his Arab neighbors and other countries, amassing a large debt. Secular (nonreligious government) states such as Saudi Arabia and Kuwait feared the Ayatollah and his Shiite threat more than Saddam Hussein's grandstanding, so they loaned money to Iraq for the war effort. Even neutral nations such as the United States had provided nonmilitary aid to help fight Iran, believing any leader had to be better than Khomeini. By 1989, Iraqi debt was estimated at $80 billion to $100 billion. Over a third of that was owed to the Kuwaitis, whose immense wealth also came from oil profits.

"UNGRATEFUL" KUWAIT

When Kuwait began to press Iraq for some payment against its debt of $32 billion, Hussein became very angry. His country was still in a terrible financial position as a result of the Iran-Iraq War, and he accused his neighbor of being ungrateful. After all, he reasoned, his people had protected the lightly defended Kuwaitis from the expansionist schemes of Iran's Ayatollah. Thirty-two billion dollars was a small payment for continued security, Hussein had argued.

Hussein was also very angry at the United Arab Emirates (UAE), a federation of small kingdoms. He thought these nations were driving down the price of oil on the world market. All of the Arab oil-producing states had formed a cooperative known as the Organization of Petroleum Exporting Countries (OPEC), so that the price of crude oil coming from the region could be controlled for the benefit of all OPEC members. Hussein accused Kuwait and the UAE of keeping the price too low by overproducing and illegally exporting beyond established quotas. His country was in dire need of revenues, but if the price for oil dropped just $1.00 per barrel, he would lose a total of $1 billion. And the price was dropping fast.

"The oil quota violators have stabbed Iraq with a poison dagger," Hussein warned in a broadcast speech. "Iraqis will not forget the saying that cutting necks is better than cutting means of living. O' God Almighty, be witness that we have warned them."

Through the summer of 1990, Hussein continued to send vitriolic messages about Kuwait. On July 18, his foreign minister, Tariq Aziz, wrote a letter to the Arab League accusing Kuwait of "systematically, deliberately and continuously harming Iraq by encroaching on its territory, stealing its oil and destroying its economy. Such behavior amounts to military aggression."[1]

Iraq was setting the stage, justifying a more aggressive stance toward its Arab neighbor. In the last act of the preliminaries, Hussein finally accused Kuwait of acting as an imperialist agent of the Western powers by overproducing to lower the price of oil and stealing oil from Iraq's own Rumaila reserves. Aziz claimed oil was stolen by drilling through the ground on a slant from Kuwaiti territory and hitting the Iraqi crude many hundreds of feet under the ground. Hussein mobilized what he claimed was a one-million-man army, the fifth largest in the world, and began sending units to Iraq's southern border along Kuwait.

WESTERN REACTION

In the United States, President George Bush's advisers were testifying in congressional hearings that the rhetoric coming out of Iraq was just posturing by Saddam Hussein. Although U.S. officials thought Hussein was hard to take at times, they believed that supporting Hussein's leadership was still crucial. Hussein was the balance against the Iranians.

On July 25, 1990, President Hussein summoned U.S. Ambassador April Glaspie to his office. Hussein spent a few minutes lecturing Ambassador Glaspie on the history of Iraq-American relations, but he soon got to the point of the meeting. He wanted to know how the United States was going to react to the disagreement with Kuwait.

"So what can it mean when America says it will now protect its friends?" asked Hussein. "It can only mean prejudice against Iraq," came his own rhetorical reply. "This stance plus maneuvers and statements which have been made has encouraged the UAE and Kuwait to disregard Iraqi rights. . . . We cannot understand the attempt to encourage some parties to harm Iraq's interests," Hussein declared.

Glaspie listened politely, then responded that the United States government was concerned about the military buildup along the border of Kuwait. She had already made it clear to Hussein that "we have no opinion on the Arab-Arab conflicts, like your border disagreement with Kuwait." But, she said, "I received an instruction to ask you, in the spirit of friendship—not in the spirit of confrontation—regarding your intentions."[2]

THE INVASION

Hussein had assured Glaspie (as well as representatives of other nations) that Iraq was not going to invade Kuwait. But on August 1, the U.S. Central Intelligence Agency told President Bush that the invasion was 90 percent likely. In spite of such warnings, the entire world reacted with great surprise when Hussein made his move in the early morning hours of August 2, 1990.

Some 100,000 Iraqi soldiers crossed the frontier and invaded Kuwait. Many of the men were from the elite Republican Guard units, and most were battle-tested veterans of the fighting with Iran. They overran the small, inept army of 20,000 Kuwaitis in about seven hours. The Iraqi borders were closed, trapping thousands of workers from India and hundreds of American and British citizens in Kuwait as well as in Iraq. Many Americans feared there would be a situation similar to the crisis during 1979–1981 when Iran held Western hostages. In the United States, people began to display yellow ribbons, as they had done to demand release of hostages in Iran, and began to call for action against Hussein, particularly when word spread about horrible atrocities against Kuwaiti civilians.

Within a week, Saddam Hussein issued an edict that annexed Kuwait to Iraq permanently. He based his action on the traditional boundaries that had existed a century before under the Ottomans. He decided to ignore the official recognition his country had given to the independent state of Kuwait in 1961 because now, as he proclaimed, the Kuwaitis had "asked" him to allow their country back into the "mother homeland." In a speech to his National Assembly, Hussein declared: "Thank God that we are now one people, one state that will be the pride of the Arabs."[3]

The Palestine Liberation Organization (PLO), a few other Arab groups, Libya, and Jordan supported Hussein's move, but the reaction of his other neighbors and the world community was clearly in opposition to this act of aggression. In this first major incident after the end of the cold war, the period from 1946 to 1989 when world politics were dominated by conflicts between the United States and the Union of Soviet Socialist Republics (USSR), a broad coalition of independent states quickly came together to condemn "the one who confronts."

Four

★

FORMING AN ALLIED COALITION

On the day of the Iraqi invasion, Sheikh Saad al-Abdulla al-Sabah, the prime minister of Kuwait, was inspecting military installations in and around Kuwait City. He recalled:

> I was thinking about the speed which with the Iraqi tanks were proceeding and their determination to enter the capital without stopping at targets or sites on the road. I realized the first priority of the criminal plot was to eliminate the legitimate leadership preparatory to eradicating Kuwait.

Sheikh Saad drove to the Dasman Palace of Emir Sheikh Jaber al-Ahmad al-Sabah and strongly urged the country's leader to move the government south. The emir eventually agreed, and the two men took a car farther away from the advancing Iraqis. They spent one night in Saad's palace, then crossed the border into Saudi Arabia. "The gap between our departure from Dasman palace and the beginning of their attack against it does not exceed half an hour," recalled the sheikh.[1]

The Saudi government was not anxious to get involved in the Kuwait-Iraq conflict, but there was soon evidence that the Iraqi forces had crossed into Saudi territory during the initial hours of the hostilities. U.S. Secretary of State James

Baker and U.S. Secretary of Defense Dick Cheney presented the latest military intelligence to the country's leader, King Fahd, in person. Satellite photographs showed that the Iraqi army was massed just north of the border, posing a possible threat to Saudi Arabian oil fields in the very near future.

For years, the Saudis had been one of America's best customers for fighter planes, tanks, and other modern weaponry. But their military still lacked the skill, experience, and numbers to mount a strong defense of their country. Presented with the evidence that his country, and perhaps all of the Middle East, was under a great threat, Fahd asked the representatives of the United States government to send troops and supplies to help defend his land.

PRESIDENT BUSH'S COALITION

Even before Fahd's request, President George Bush had taken action. The day following the invasion, he announced that "this aggression will not stand." Using his emergency powers, he signed executive orders freezing Iraqi assets that were located in the United States and barring trade between the two countries. He also put U.S. military around the world on full alert and sent ships steaming toward the Persian Gulf.

His most important action was to call the leaders of nations throughout the world in an attempt to create a unified response to Saddam Hussein's outlaw activity. Many countries had expressed outrage upon hearing of the invasion, and President Bush decided to use the United Nations to bring the most pressure to bear on Iraq. With the support of Mikhail Gorbachev of the Soviet Union, which was cooperating for the first time since World War II as an ally of the United States, the United Nations' Security Council eventually passed twelve resolutions on Iraq's invasion of Kuwait.

The first, Resolution 660, stated that the Security Council was "alarmed by the invasion of Kuwait of 2 August 1990 by the military forces of Iraq." Declaring that there was "a breach of international peace and security," the resolution condemned the Iraqi invasion of Kuwait and demanded that "Iraq withdraw immediately and unconditionally all its forces to the positions in which they were located on 1 August 1990."[2]

Five days later, Resolution 661 was favorably voted, creating an embargo on the transfer of goods to or from the "outlaw state." All member states supported the trade ban on the "import into their territories of all commodities and products originating in Iraq or Kuwait exported therefrom after the date of the present resolution."[3] Only such humanitarian goods as medical supplies and food were exempt from the embargo.

Immediately thereafter, Turkey shut down the great oil pipeline that transported the bulk of Iraq's oil out of the country to the world market. The United States Navy established a blockade in the Persian Gulf and began to stop merchant vessels coming from or going to ports that might be involved in Iraqi trade. With the economic isolation of Iraq almost completed, the deployment of military personnel and equipment picked up speed. British Prime Minister Margaret Thatcher advocated a multinational response, adding Britain's considerable support to the effort, while President Bush spent hours on the phone getting commitments from many other world leaders. The coalition was coming together.

Bush deftly put into action his plan, code-named Desert Shield. In a matter of months he had brought together the greatest force of arms and men and women since the Vietnam era to stand against an enemy army. The United States was forced to make economic, political, and military

U.S. Navy vessels blockading the Persian Gulf prevent
a merchant vessel (center) *from going to an Iraqi port.*

promises to many countries, but the outcome was an unprecedented coalition of nations, some with opposing interests and goals, which was the basis for what President Bush called the New World Order. "A partnership based on consultation, cooperation, and collective action" is how he described it in a speech to the United Nations.[4]

Within three months the speediest deployment in U.S. history took place, with tens of thousands of land, sea, and air forces sent to Saudi Arabia. By mid-January 1991, a twenty-eight-nation coalition had amassed thousands of aircraft (both helicopters and fighter planes), hundreds of tanks, and millions of pounds of equipment. A total of forty nations eventually allied against Iraq, but some supplied medical personnel or hospitals rather than weapons and troops and/or pledged billions of dollars to support what now appeared to be an imminent war. A ground force of

President Bush addressing the United Nations regarding the coalition against Iraq

more than 600,000 troops was poised to fight a force of 545,000 Iraqis. Most of these troops—527,000 men and women—were from the United States.

WOMEN AT WAR

For the first time in the twentieth century the United States was prepared to fight a war with an all-volunteer army. This army's makeup was very different from that of previous military forces. In the modern military, women trained alongside their male counterparts in most cases, and approximately 32,000 women were sent to Saudi Arabia. They were responsible for performing many crucial tasks, including the dangerous work of flying helicopters to ferry supplies, ammunition, and men to forward positions. U.S. law prohibited placing women in combat positions, although with long-

A U.S. Army MP stands guard with her
M-60 machine gun during the Persian Gulf War.

range missiles, the front lines could have shifted quickly, making the law ineffective.

Military women in Saudi Arabia also faced other prohibitions. According to Molly Moore, senior military correspondent for the *Washington Post*, "Many American military units delayed sending women to the Gulf for fear they would offend the Saudis, whose Muslim culture severely restricted the activities of women." Muslim women, for example, were not allowed to drive cars, were required to wear clothing that completely covered their bodies, and were segregated from men. As Moore reported:

> Most restaurants required women to eat behind partitions in the back while men sat in the more elegant main dining area. Some refused to serve women at all. One day I walked into three different restaurants before I found one willing to serve me lunch—and then the proprietor would only give me takeout.
>
> The segregation did not stop at the lunch counter, however. Women in Saudi Arabia had to sit in the rear of the public buses, stand in separate lines from men in airports, and enter most public buildings through the back doors.

Moore found that many American military women were frustrated and exasperated by the Islamic rules governing women, who are considered sacred but also likely to tempt men, particularly if women's bare flesh is revealed or if they have close contact with men in public. Even in 120°F heat, American military women in public were not allowed to wear shorts and were forced to wear long-sleeved shirts.

Finally, however, some concessions were made. "At the insistence of U.S. commanders, women were allowed to drive military vehicles in the line of duty. And for the first time, the Saudi Air Force opened its $80 million gymnasium complex at the Dhahran air base to women. The women could even use the Olympic-sized swimming pool if they wore baggy shirts and knee-length shorts for swimsuits," Moore reported.[5]

Five

★

IGH-TECH AIR WAR

On November 29, 1990, the United Nations passed Resolution 678. It authorized "member states cooperating with the Government of Kuwait . . . to use all necessary means to uphold and implement [the Security Council] Resolution 660 and all subsequent relevant resolutions and to restore international peace and security in the area."[1]

This resolution was pushed through the international body by the United States. It told Saddam Hussein that he was facing an absolute deadline of forty-five days from the time the resolutions were issued to comply with demands to withdraw and to return the kingdom he had illegally annexed.

International forces in Saudi Arabia began to train in earnest. Their commander and the overall strategist for the plan to free Kuwait was United States General Norman Schwarzkopf.

The general was given responsibility for the operation because of a plan he had developed some time before. He speculated that Kuwait was in a vulnerable position, and he had decided to work out a scenario for the defense of Saudi Arabia should an aggressor overrun its neighbor nation. Little did he realize that his plan would actually be put into effect in such a short time.

REACTION AT HOME

In the United States, Congress debated whether to autho-
rize the use of force against Hussein and his army. Some
members of Congress balked at the huge number of troops
assembled. Even though General Schwarzkopf said he
would never be put in the position of those who were in
command during the Vietnam War, some were very fearful
that this war, like Vietnam, would be lengthy and cost many
lives.

"In the long run," said Senator John Kerry of Massa-
chusetts, "such a war could lead to renewed terrorist attacks
on Americans as a result of our having killed innumerable
Arab citizens." And Senator Barbara Boxer of California
noted that "I had a community meeting in my district. . . . A
thousand people came out. I have never seen anything like it.
We voted . . . on how they would vote on a resolution to go to
war, and 95 percent voted no."[2]

Many Americans thought the economic sanctions
should be given more time to work. Some evidence indicated
that Iraq was beginning to suffer from lack of basic necessi-
ties because of the U.N.-sanctioned and U.S.-enforced
embargo. And there were some voices raised about the
morality of committing troops and resources to secure a
nation that had shown very little progress toward democracy
over the years.

Five weeks after American troops were deployed to
Saudi Arabia, the executive committee of the National
Council of Churches called for a public debate in regard to
U.S. intentions in the gulf and asked: "Will U.S. intervention
assure the return of the ruling family to power in Kuwait?
Will the U.S. seek to guarantee the Kuwaitis' right to self-
determination and representative government? Or is the

An antiwar demonstration in San Francisco, January 1991

goal of this military action preeminently the protection of U.S. access to oil supplies?"[3]

Other critics contended that the war could not be justified on moral grounds. War in the Middle East "risks engulfing the region in volatility, bitterness, ecological disaster, the possible use of chemical and nuclear weapons, and violence that will only multiply and reverberate around the Middle East and the world," argued Jim Wallis, editor of the religious magazine *Sojourners* and pastor of the Sojourners community in Washington, D.C. The fact that "U.S. troops are disproportionately people of color reflects the moral injustice of this nation's continued racial polarization," Wallis contended. "It is a moral contradiction that young people, whose door to a better life is closed at home, have been promised an open door to the future through military careers and education only to see that open door now become a pathway to killing or being killed."[4]

Public opinion polls consistently showed that more than half the African-Americans surveyed were against a war in the Gulf, while eight out of every ten whites favored the military buildup. But a vast majority of Americans began to accept the view of President Bush and his administration that Hussein was the equivalent of Adolf Hitler, the evil Nazi dictator who initiated World War II.

Those in favor of armed conflict against Hussein were particularly horrified with stories about Iraqi atrocities, including the rape, torture, and mass execution of Kuwaiti citizens. In fact, former United Nations Ambassador Jeane Kirkpatrick declared that Saddam Hussein needed to be punished "to deter future aggressors from similar violence and make the world safer for all."[5]

Secretary of State James Baker offered another reason to prepare for war against Hussein: economics. Baker contended that

> the economic lifeline of the industrial world runs from the Gulf, and we cannot permit a dictator such as this to sit astride that economic lifeline. To bring it down to the level of the average American citizen, let me say that means jobs.[6]

Jobs, however, were not a deciding factor for most Americans and Europeans who wanted tough actions against Hussein. Rather, it was the kind of reasoning offered by such leaders as Prime Minister Margaret Thatcher, who said,

"Iraq's invasion of Kuwait defies every principle for which the United Nations stands. If we let it succeed, no small country can ever feel safe again. The law of the jungle would take over from the rule of law."[7]

As the Desert Shield buildup continued and after the war began, great numbers of Americans, regardless of skin color or economic status, joined marches and rallies, waving flags and wearing yellow ribbons, in support of the Persian Gulf War. And after much soul-searching debate, Congress finally voted on January 12, 1991, to allow the president to eject Iraqi forces from Kuwait if the January 15 deadline was not met. The vote in the House was 250–183, and in the Senate it was 52–47. Last-minute talks held between Secretary of State Baker and Iraq's Tariq Aziz had already broken down. The Iraqis were not willing to budge. January 15 came and went, and the world held its breath.

FIRE IN THE SKY

Operation Desert Storm began almost nineteen hours after the midnight deadline had passed, and millions of Americans were able to see the first effects on the CNN TV broadcast from Baghdad. The results of the allied air attack were riveting. Everyone, it seemed, watched the war coverage.

Many Americans, preparing for bed that night, had difficulty sleeping. What would this lead to? Would Iraq launch countermeasures against the United States?

"I had such a stomachache that first night," recalled Michelle Sandoval. She and the patrons at her Ojai, California, restaurant had spent the entire evening watching the CNN broadcast of events in Baghdad, Saudi Arabia, and Washington, D.C. "I mean, it was sort of like watching a video game . . . it was unreal in so many respects. There must have been people getting killed in front of our eyes on the other side of the world. But here we were watching like this was just another game show."[8]

The air strikes were very real, of course. Besides the U.S. Army and Marine Apache helicopters that took out the radar installations that night, the ultimate in high-technology weaponry was in the sky over Iraq and Kuwait. The goal for the 750 sorties flown in the first seven hours was to clear a "flight corridor," or a path that planes would use later to reach their primary targets.

EF-111 Ravens and F-4G Wild Weasels were the first to go in after the Apaches, clearing the way through the antiaircraft systems by "jamming" the electronics of the Iraqis' controls. Right on their tails were the remarkable Black Jets. Also nicknamed the Nighthawks, these F-117 Stealth fighters made it to Baghdad virtually undetected because the $100 million aircraft was especially designed to be invisible to radar.

This F-117A Stealth fighter on its way to
the Middle East is refueled in the air.

This light bomber was a big question mark before the Gulf War. It had not been tested in combat. But Air Force Captain Rob Donaldson knew what his plane could do on the flight to downtown Baghdad. As Donaldson reported: "Since the airplane is black and sinister looking and flew at night, the Saudis called us Shaba. That means, 'a ghost who walks at night and is not seen.' They were terrified of the airplane because they don't like the night."[9]

If the Saudis were terrified of the F-117, imagine what the Iraqis must have been feeling about this nightmare over their skies—unseen but always on target with its devastating bombs. Captain Donaldson recalled that

> The 117s were the only aircraft allowed to go downtown to Baghdad because of our capability to get there undetected as well as deliver [laser]-guided munitions. They reduced civilian casualties and collateral damage by sending us.
>
> I attacked with a dual door drop, released both bombs almost at the same time, and the jet jumped like a racing horse when those 4000 pounds dropped away. As I looked through the display about two seconds before my bombs impacted, I saw two other bombs explode. My bombs hit just as many others went off, which gives you a clue to the number of aircraft we had going through the same sky at the same time.[10]

Command and Control targets were the first to get blown apart during the initial bombing runs, which also included planes from the portion of Kuwait not under Iraqi control, Saudi Arabia, and Great Britain.

Another high-tech weapon that added to the terrible punch against the Iraqis' ability to conduct war was the Tomahawk cruise missile. These one-and-a-half-ton unmanned rocket bombs were launched from ships in the

A Tomahawk cruise missile is launched from a U.S. Navy vessel.

Persian Gulf or Arabian Sea or from aircraft such as the F-15Es and F-18s. With a range of 1,500 miles, these $1 million missiles are like robot planes, delivering a thousand-pound payload with deadly accuracy. They fly low, under radar where possible, and create a lot of destruction.

In the United States and other parts of the world, people saw and heard early morning video reports by leaders of multinational forces, who explained that the night raids had gone even better than they had expected. Military officials displayed videotapes shot from cameras mounted on the bombers that had taken part in the attack. The playback showed the awesome accuracy and power of this latest generation of weapons being used against Hussein's forces. In one case, a "smart" bomb appeared to find its way down a tall air shoot of an Iraqi command center, and seconds later the walls of that structure exploded outward in four directions simultaneously.

The multinational commanders were all smiles, and people at home began to hope the war would soon end. But where was the highly prized Iraqi Air Force during the attack in the skies over its land? Could the "one who confronts" be up to some trick that no one could figure out? Time would tell.

Six

★

ATTACKS AND COUNTERATTACKS

On January 18, television broadcasts showed the second night of air raids against the Iraqis. B-52 bombers, the thirty-year-old workhorses of the Vietnam War, were now brought into the action, dropping hundreds of tons of explosives on Saddam Hussein's elite fighting unit, the Republican Guard. These men were massed on both sides of the Iraq-Kuwait border and were targeted because of their legendary fighting ability. If there was to be a ground assault later, General Schwarzkopf did not want the Guard to be at full strength.

News anchors in TV home studios were analyzing these events and speculating on what countermeasures the Iraqis might take when reporters on the ground in remote locations started scrambling to take cover and find gas masks. As people watched their television screens, air raid sirens could be heard in the background. Saudi Arabia and Israel were under attack from incoming missiles. Many thought that this was the chemical or germ warfare response everyone in the multinational force had been fearing.

One Scud rocket, a product of the Soviet Union's armaments factories with a range of nearly 750 miles, was on its way to Saudi Arabia. Eight others were over Israeli airspace. Although the Scuds were not accurate enough to be directed at military targets, their use against civilian populations struck fear into those in their paths. This was especially true in Israel, where Hussein had threatened to destroy half of the country with chemical weapons. Just before the assault Hussein had also broadcast a directive to Arabs everywhere to begin terrorist attacks against the invaders and initiate the "mother of all battles."

The Scud over Saudi Arabia was knocked out of the sky by an antimissile missile known as the Patriot. When the alarm was sounded, a U.S. crew supported by the missile command unit (MICOM) set the homing mechanism on the Patriot and blew the Scud to pieces.

ISRAEL'S ROLE

Israel, however, was not protected by the MICOM gunners; no Patriots were deployed there. The eight Scuds that came in from positions on the Jordan-Iraq border fell on Tel Aviv and Haifa. At least a dozen people were injured in the explosions, but, fortunately, there was no poison gas in the payload.

Israeli military units, already on full alert, prepared to strike back. Israel had earned a reputation for hitting back hard when it was attacked, and this incident struck at the heart of its security. But now George Bush had to convince the Israeli government to stay out of the fight, something the nation had not done before.

Saddam Hussein had attacked Israel for one reason only: Arab states all around Israel were sworn enemies of the Jewish nation. Hussein hoped that by prodding Israel to attack Iraq, the three Arab nations that had joined the multinational force against him would have to pull out of the fight. Those nations, Hussein believed, would not tolerate Israel's act against another Arab state. Hussein speculated the entire coalition would crumble if he could get Israel to react.

In late January 1991, Iraq launched Scud missiles against Israel and heavily damaged areas of Tel Aviv.

With the approval of President Bush, Deputy Secretary of State Lawrence Eagleburger promised the Israelis that the United States would immediately deploy Patriot missile launchers to Israel and that the subsequent air strikes would target Scud installations on Iraqi soil. The next day the Patriots began arriving, even as more Scud rockets smashed into Israeli homes and businesses. Yet Israel waited, reserving the right to attack later if the government felt it was necessary. Instead, civil defense units throughout the country began distributing gas masks to as many of their citizens as they could reach. They also provided directions on how to seal a room in the home to be used in case of an Iraqi gas or chemical bomb attack. Much of this was shown on TV in the United States.

The random way in which the Scuds fell meant that no one could really know where the next one might land. And even if the newly arrived Patriots could hit them in the air, Hussein's chemical warheads might not be destroyed. So for the next six weeks, much of the Israeli populace spent most of its time in or around the sealed rooms.

Robert Werman was an American Jew who had emigrated to Israel in 1967 to become a citizen of that country. On January 19, 1991, his sealed room was prepared, but he was not ready to just hide there quietly. Using a computer and a modem, he began to post messages to the outside world via a computer network. His writings were eventually distributed to the far ends of the earth along the Internet, and he began to receive hundreds of responses each day from people who wanted to learn about the more human side of this war rather than what the popular media was providing them. Werman was happy to oblige.

> Saturday, 19 January: The Third Attack. After two nights of air-raid sirens, jumping up to get to a sealed room, putting on gas masks. Two real ones so far; two false alarms. A bit tiring—but relief that the weapons are conventional, and that so few people are seriously hurt.
>
> Schools were closed on Thursday and will remain closed. Since both parents work in Israel, one will have to stay home. Meanwhile, most nonessential industries and stores are closed. The Patriot missiles that the U.S. is giving us will be too late and too few.

The big question is, Does Saddam have chemical warheads on his missiles? There is little doubt that he will use them if he has.

The elimination of the missile launchers seems a difficult if not impossible task. Generally, morale seems high. People are told to stay close to home, to have gas masks ready. They, for the most part, listen to instructions.[1]

OIL SPILLS AND FIRES

Besides the random Scud attacks that did very little damage to civilian or military targets, Hussein's response to the continual allied bombardment seemed to be one of hiding. The nearly 2,000 sorties that went out of Saudi Arabia or Turkey or from the surrounding gulfs were rarely met with any Iraqi jets. As a matter of fact, Hussein had ordered his air force hidden in camouflaged hangars or flown to neighboring Iran for safekeeping. And most of his tanks were kept in bunkers to protect them from the ever-present allied bombers.

He had no defensive strategy, except for a desperate plan unleashed during the second week of the war. Millions of barrels of crude oil were released into the Persian Gulf off Kuwait's refinery at Mina al Ahmadi. Militarily, the oil spill did nothing and was eventually stopped, but it created an ecological disaster, devastating plant and animal life in the region.

Carrying out another of Hussein's plans, the Iraqi army set fire to hundreds of Kuwaiti oil wells, causing heavy black smoke to rise miles into the air all across the desert. Hussein hoped to cloud the skies over Kuwait so that planes would have a difficult time approaching Iraqi positions. The fires would burn for many weeks until teams from the United States could be brought over to douse them. Although the

*Red Adair oil well fire-fighters were part of the teams brought
from the United States to extinguish the fires started by the Iraqi army.*

plan was a military failure, the black smoke and fires created
some problems for pilots.

Marine First Lieutenant Lance "Jolt" Hoyt was on a mission in his F/A-18 Hornet attack jet over the Kuwaiti oil
fields on February 17. The weather was very bad with heavy
cloud cover, but he was looking for "a lucrative target 20
miles south of Kuwait City." He remembered, "It was reported to be 30 to 40 tanks out in the open . . . a nice juicy little
target."

He and a buddy, C. J., were each going to fly in under the clouds to see if the target was really there before command sent in another dozen jets to take on the tanks. They were underneath the clouds

> at about 900 feet but were over the area of burning oil wells . . . the air was full of real black, smoky haze from the oil fires. . . . We were being illuminated by all those fires. I remember looking up through the top of the canopy and seeing the shadow of my jet moving across the cloud deck—that's how bright it was.

After a great deal of searching, C. J. finally dropped his bombs on a truck convoy. The tanks were nowhere to be found. "I watched where his bombs detonated and aimed for his explosions," recalled Hoyt. But a second later he looked up to realize that he had flown into a trap.

> I looked over and saw a four set stream of tracers aimed in front of and a little bit above me. It was a real, *real*, close range shot. . . . He held the trigger down like he was going to empty everything he had at me! . . . I pushed full forward on the stick to fly underneath the stream of bullets. I could hear the sonic crack as they went over the canopy and really thought they were going to make holes in my vertical tail.

After maneuvering away from the first Iraqi jet he came out face-to-face with another Iraqi pilot only 150 feet above the ground. When the enemy opened fire, Hoyt

> saw the burst coming straight at the nose of the airplane . . . so I racked into a six-G level turn to the right. . . . I was level with some of the oil fires . . . and ended up flying straight past a couple of the fires to try and hide in there. I grabbed

a quick look around, didn't see any more triple-A [antiair-craft fire], and decided I'd had enough. I hit the blowers and stood the jet straight up to punch through as many cloud layers as I could before I ran out of airspeed.[2]

DISCRIMINATION IN THE UNITED STATES

Even as the U.S. and coalition forces were waging successful raids over Iraq, some Americans were reacting in highly prejudicial ways against those of Arab ancestry in the United States. At one California high school, for example, students put up a sign in the parking lot declaring: NUKE IRAQ! KILL ALL THE TOWEL HEADS! According to a news report, "Anti-Middle Eastern epithets, jokes and other remarks, fueled by the Persian Gulf War, were widely heard in the hallways [of the Huntington Beach school]."

In Los Angeles County, hate crimes against Arabs and Muslims "increased substantially as a result of the Gulf War," and others such as Latinos and Armenians who supposedly "look like Arabs" were harassed as well, according to Eugene S. Mornell, executive director of the Commission on Human Relations in Los Angeles County. In an opinion piece for the *Los Angeles Times*, Mornell noted that the thousands of Arab Americans and Muslim Americans

in this county reflect as much diversity of background and opinion as any ethnic or religious group among us. Many have escaped problems of the Middle East to seek freedom and opportunity in this country. Most are understandably concerned about the war. All have the same rights and protections as any other American.[3]

In Detroit, Michigan, where there is a large population of Arab Americans, some also became victims of hate crimes. Once the Gulf War broke out and even weeks after hostilities ended, they were cursed at or their businesses were vandalized or burned or threatened with bombings. In order to prevent damage to their property, some Arab Americans felt they had to proclaim their loyalty to the United States by flying American flags or hanging yellow ribbons. They also held news conferences to explain to other citizens what Arab Americans were all about. A few weeks after the end of the war Basil Boji, who emigrated from Iraq to the United States in 1961, told a reporter: "I am an American. I chose to come here. I have worked hard here to build up my business. This is my country, and I am loyal to my country."[4]

Seven

★

*T*HE GROUND WAR

On February 9, the Soviet Union's leader, Mikhail Gorbachev, openly questioned the way the war was being conducted by the multinational coalition. His country still supported the goal of getting Iraq to leave Kuwait, and his emissaries urged Hussein to do so. But the Soviets were concerned that much of the damage being done to Iraq's infrastructure and its civilian population was unjustified. In Morocco, thousands of Arabs had also taken to the streets protesting the American action. Gorbachev started working hard to broker a peace agreement that would be acceptable to all parties.

After several days of meetings between Iraqi and Soviet diplomats, there was an announcement that the Iraqis would be willing to withdraw from Kuwait if Israel was also forced to withdraw from Palestinian territories that the Arab nations felt had been illegally annexed to Israel. The proposed agreement also dismissed Iraqi payment for damages that Kuwait suffered due to the invasion. But these two conditions were totally unacceptable to President Bush and his advisers.

Another attempt by the Soviets also fell short, and the United States started looking for an opening to launch a ground attack that would utterly destroy Hussein's army.

General Norman Schwarzkopf (left), *commander of U.S. forces in the Gulf, confers with General Colin Powell* (right), *chairman of the Joint Chiefs of Staff.*

Chairman of the Joint Chiefs of Staff Colin Powell suggested that Hussein be given an ultimatum in order to move events along, especially after it was learned that he had set the Kuwaiti oil fields afire.

On Friday, February 22, President Bush decided to act, and from the White House lawn he spoke to the world. "The coalition will give Saddam Hussein until noon Saturday," he warned, "to do what he must do, to begin his immediate and unconditional withdrawal from Kuwait."[1]

Hussein's response was to send the sixteenth Scud missile flying toward Israel and another into Saudi Arabia. Both fell in unoccupied areas. Then, as the deadline passed at noon on February 23, Baghdad came under one of the most intense attacks to date from coalition planes. In Kuwait,

1,200 missions were flown, with bombers targeting Iraqi troop positions. That day, a total of almost 3,000 raids were made over enemy airspace.

THE GROUND ATTACK

The actual time of day when troops on the ground began moving against Iraqi positions is not clear. But by early Sunday morning in Saudi Arabia, the first shots were being fired. Hussein had expected the brunt of the attack to come from positions along the Saudi-Kuwait border, and well-designed trenches had been established there. But the air attacks had decimated the defenders, who no longer had adequate food, water, or the other basics of survival. The American marines who led the incursion into Kuwait found little resistance, and by midnight they had moved twenty miles toward Kuwait City.

This maneuver was part of a bluff, however. Along the Kuwaiti coast, 150,000 Iraqi troops were dug in, waiting for the attack that was never to come. As part of the ploy to keep these soldiers in their positions, 18,000 marines were in the Gulf preparing for what looked to be an amphibious landing. While Hussein's forces were looking east and south, General Schwarzkopf's multinational team was sweeping around to the west where a French, American, and Saudi attack quickly took the village and airfield of As Salman some fifty miles inside Iraq. Within the first ten hours of the ground offensive, some 5,500 Iraqi soldiers became prisoners of war. The half-starved troops were even surrendering to teams of news reporters—anyone, it seemed, who might get them out of harm's way and to a decent meal.

The advance of the coalition forces was almost nonstop for the first three days with very few casualties among these troops. In contrast, Iraqis were being killed handily where they gave any resistance. One Iraqi soldier, Sadar, who had been drafted into the army and cared little about the reasons for the war, was part of the pack of fleeing Iraqis. Since there were few vehicles operating, he bribed a man with a car to help him escape. Sadar reported:

> As we were driving along, we could see two big lorries [flat-bed trucks], Iraqi military lorries that had just been hit. They'd been bombed . . . totally destroyed. It was chaotic. We drove very fast in between the two burning lorries. . . . I saw with my own two eyes, there were two people trapped in the cab of one of the lorries and there were flames all around them. As we drove past . . . I didn't know what to think. I just wanted to get away from that terrible scene.[2]

In many cases, Iraqi soldiers threw down their weapons and gave up. And there was some concern at one point that dealing with the huge numbers of prisoners of war (POWs)

Iraqi prisoners of war

would necessitate a slowdown in the rapid advance of the allies. But advance they did, with the help of air support that bombed all of the bridges over the Euphrates River, which was the only way back to Baghdad. The noose began to tighten on the elite fighters of the Republican Guard.

PERILS OF WAR

During this phase of the fighting, an Air Force F-16 fighter plane supporting the ground troops' advance went down behind enemy lines. A search-and-rescue helicopter carrying eight Americans went deep into Iraq to find the pilot of the F-16. On board the helicopter was Major Rhonda Cornum, an Army doctor stationed in Saudi Arabia. Though women were denied access to frontline positions by U.S. law, it was often the case in the Gulf War that women were willing to place themselves in the line of fire.

"We were flying fast and low," wrote Major Cornum, "so low that the pilot of our helicopter had to pull up to fly over the convoy of American trucks streaming through Iraq." She noted that:

> It was another chilly gray afternoon, February 27, 1991, the fourth day of the ground war. . . . I remember crossing over a convoy and seeing American vehicles with inverted Vs painted on the sides and tops. . . . We waved to the troops bundled up in their bulky chemical gear, and they waved back at us. The air was filled with smoke and soot from oil fires. . . . About forty-five seconds after we passed over the last American vehicle, and without warning, green tracers began streaking up at us from the ground, while I heard the crack-crack of weapons firing. . . . I heard something big hit the aircraft and I knew it wasn't doing well. . . . Everything went black.[3]

Major Cornum survived the wreck with two broken arms and a smashed knee. Five of the crew were killed instantly. She and her two companions were captured by Republican Guard soldiers and thrown into cells. Fortunately, she was soon released because a cease-fire was called by President Bush just a few hours later.

THE END OF THE FIGHTING

The last battle of the war was really a massacre of the surrounded Republican Guard units and those Iraqi defenders who were making a run for the north. Captain David Pierson served as the battalion intelligence officer of a tank squad called the Tuskers. His recollection of the final battle gives a picture of what the devastation was like.

According to the captain, on the last day of the ground war a sandstorm began to blow and visibility was almost zero. "Thermal sites on board the tanks . . . were able to see through the surrounding dust to locate their prey. Sporadic fire broke out as the surprised and confused Iraqis opened fire. Suddenly, the storm stopped and the dust settled to the ground. Both sides could now see each other." But as the Iraqis tried to fight back and move out of the trap the next morning, the captain's unit reformed and refueled. Then they continued

> toward the Republican Guard fleeing from the onslaught of VII Corps. . . . Around 1500 hours the Division ran into a large Iraqi armored unit moving west along Highway 8. The Tuskers set up in a hasty defense while the artillery pounded the approaching enemy. The barrage continued throughout the evening and into the morning. A ceasefire was scheduled to go into effect at 0500 hours and the artillery picked up the pace shortly before the deadline. Suddenly

the guns stopped firing and an eerie silence fell across the battlefield.

The next day everyone thought the fighting was over, but during a radio transmission that morning, one of the forward scout positions reported that remnants of Iraqi divisions—tanks and infantry fighting vehicles—were heading toward them. Pierson reported:

> The scouts were fired upon by Sagger anti-tank missiles and a Rocket Propelled Grenade. They returned the fire and then overran the Iraqi position. The Iraqi armored column turned to the north. They were moving into a peninsula area of the [Rumaylah] Oilfields that led to a causeway bridge across the marshes of the Euphrates River. . . . Ten minutes later we were rolling. We reached a reserve position and stopped in place.

According to Pierson, new scout reports put the number of fleeing vehicles at more than one hundred, "both tracked and wheeled, lined up on the road facing north in a desperate traffic jam." Before the Tuskers could take action, AH-64 Apache helicopters flew overhead in an attack pattern, systematically destroying the vehicles. "Iraqi soldiers, seeing the vehicles in front of them explode one at a time, scrambled out of their iron coffins and abandoned them on the road. Panic spread down the line of vehicles as hundreds of soldiers fled" from the attacking helicopters. "With munitions expended and fuel running low, the Apaches pulled off station leaving 102 burning hulks in their wake." Yet the Iraqis continued to resist, and later on that day, Pierson

> rode with the battalion executive officer to the causeway. As we approached I could hardly believe my eyes. Stretching

This convoy of Iraqis fleeing to Basrah was destroyed by U.S. forces shortly before the end of the war.

before me, as far as the eye could see, was a line of charred and abandoned vehicles lined up bumper to bumper. . . .

I walked for over a mile out onto the land bridge and the destruction never ceased. I stopped and opened the cab of a truck to be confronted by a charred corpse still grasping the steering wheel—still manning his post for the drive into the nether world. I gazed at the carnage and shook my head. All this waste, all these lives lost—for what? The legacy of a madman to be rebuilt and destroyed again by my sons a decade from now. It's never over.[4]

Indeed, some Americans have that opinion today. Certainly the stated objectives of the war were accomplished and Kuwait again became an independent nation. However, the great flush of pride and power that Americans felt after the successful Persian Gulf War began to fade when they realized that the cease-fire brought no real solutions to long-standing conflicts in the Middle East.

In 1996, Saddam Hussein was still in power, and since the end of the war, he has led ruthless and brutal attacks against some of his own citizens as well as family members who rebelled against his dictatorship. Just after the cease-fire, for example, the Kurds who lived in the province of Kurdistan in northern Iraq rose up against Hussein. Encouraged by the United States and other Western nations, in March 1991 the Kurds attacked Hussein's Security Headquarters in one town, killing numerous security police. But Hussein soon sent troops to avenge the killings, and hundreds of thousands of Kurds fled over the mountains in a convoy of lorries, trucks, cars, and other vehicles; many were on foot, trying to find safety in Iran.

Fourteen-year-old Mustaffa Aziz and his family were among the refugees, and Mustaffa reported that their lorry was quickly filled with about fifty people. As they traveled toward the mountains, they heard the sound of helicopters. Mustaffa recalled that "people got really confused . . . because they didn't know whether it would be the Iraqi army [or] the Americans coming to help us . . . [or] the United Nations." The helicopter turned toward the mountains and, Mustaffa reported, "we knew straight away. We saw the Iraqi flag on the tail of the helicopter . . . so everybody started to panic. And there was this bright light, a little smoke coming out, and this red thing was just flying towards the mountain. It hit the cars."

The helicopter fired on the convoy several times, and it

turned around and came back to strafe the refugees with gunfire again. In Mustaffa's words, "All you see was women grabbing onto their children and you know, dragging them along . . . people literally just leaving their cars, leaving all their belongings in their cars, just running towards the mountains."[5] During one strafing incident, Mustaffa's mother was killed by a runaway car. But Mustaffa and the rest of his family eventually reached safety across the mountains and went to Great Britain to live.

Besides murdering thousands of fleeing Iraqis, Hussein also made plans for massive global destruction. He was preparing to produce nuclear and biological weapons—until the United Nations uncovered these diabolical operations. In addition, two of Saddam Hussein's sons-in-law, who defected to Jordan and denounced Hussein, returned to Iraq in February 1996 and were promptly murdered by clansmen. Two of Hussein's grandsons were also killed. Thus, many people worldwide have questioned whether Hussein will again become a threat. One can only hope that nations everywhere will heed the advice of General Schwarzkopf, hero of the Gulf War, who in 1991 urged the nation to pursue peace as vigorously as it fought the war.

Source Notes

One

1. Transcript of videotape, *Desert Storm: The War Begins* (Cable News Network, Turner Home Entertainment), 1991.

2. Michael Kelly, *Martyrs' Day: Chronicle of a Small War* (New York: Random House, 1993), 63–64.

3. Lt. Gen. Edward M. Flanagan Jr., *Lightning: The 101st in the Gulf War* (Washington, D.C.: Brassey's, Inc., 1994) 115.

Two

1. Quoted in Alan Geyer and Barbara G. Green, *Lines in the Sand: Justice and the Gulf War* (Louisville, Ky.: Westminster/John Knox Press, 1992), 35.

2. Judith Miller and Laurie Mylroie, *Saddam Hussein and the Crisis in the Gulf* (New York: Times Books, 1990), 31.

3. Elaine Sciolino, *The Outlaw State* (New York: John Wiley, 1991), 63.

Three

1. Transcript, *Desert Storm: The War Begins.*

2. Ofra Bengio, *Saddam Speaks on the Gulf Crisis: A Collection of Documents* (Tel-Aviv: The Moshe Dayan Center for Middle Eastern and African Studies, 1992), 99–107.

3. James Ridgeway, ed., *The March to War* (New York: Four Walls Eight Windows, 1991), 61.

Four

1. <http://www.yahoo.com> Reuters Online, Tuesday, August 1, 1995, 8:42 A.M.

2. Quoted in electronic file <http://www.nd.edu/~aleyden/>

3. Ibid.

4. Transcript, *Desert Storm: The War Begins.*

5. Molly Moore, *A Woman at War* (New York: Charles Scribner's Sons, 1993), 31–33.

Five

1. Quoted in electronic file <http://www.nd.edu/~aleyden/>

2. Quoted in James F. Dunnigan and Austin Bay, *From Shield to Storm* (New York: William Morrow and Company, 1992), 140.

3. Geyer and Green, *Lines in the Sand*, 67.

4. Quoted in James Turner Johnson and George Weigel, *Just War and the Gulf War* (Lanham, Md.: University Press of America, 1991), 148, 150.

5. Quoted in Michael J. Mazarr, Don M. Snider, and James A. Blackwell Jr., *Desert Storm: The Gulf War and What We Learned* (Boulder, Colo.: Westview Press, 1993), 72.

6. Quoted in Lawrence Freedman and Efraim Karsh, *The Gulf Conflict, 1990–1991 Diplomacy and War in the New World Order.* (Princeton, N.J.: Princeton University Press, 1993), 224.

7. Ibid., 111.

8. Personal interview with Martin Gay, June 13, 1995.

9. Quoted in Ed Herlick, *Separated by War* (Blue Ridge Summit, Pa.: Tab Books, 1994), 207.

10. Ibid., 213.

Six

1. Robert Werman, *Notes from a Sealed Room* (Carbondale, Ill.: Southern Illinois University Press, 1993), 19.

2. Herlick, *Separated by War,* 169–172.

3. Eugene S. Mornell, "Letter to the Editor," *Los Angeles Times*, February 3, 1991, Opinion Section, 6.

4. Quoted in Amy Harmon, "No-Win Predicament of Iraqi-Immigrant Merchants in Detroit," *Los Angeles Times*, March 16, 1991, 1.

Seven

1. Transcript from videotape. *Desert Storm: Victory* (Cable News Network, Turner Home Entertainment), 1991.

2. "The Gulf War," Fifth Anniversary, PBS, *Frontline* broadcast, January 9–10, 1996. Electronic posting "Voices in the Storm" <http://www.pbs.org/pages/frontline/gulf/voices>

3. Rhonda Cornum and Peter Copeland, *She Went to War: The Rhonda Cornum Story* (Novato, Calif.: Presidio Press, 1992), 1–10.

4. CPT David Pierson, "Into the Valley," *Tracings in the Sand*, <http://www.pbs.org/pages/frontline/gulf/voices>

5. "The Gulf War," Fifth Anniversary, PBS, *Frontline* broadcast, January 9–10, 1996. Electronic posting "Voices in the Storm" <http://www.pbs.org/pages/frontline/gulf/voices>

For Further Information

Books

Bratman, Fred. *War in the Persian Gulf.* Brookfield, Conn.: Millbrook Press, 1992.

Cipkowski, Peter. *Understanding the Crisis in the Persian Gulf.* New York: John Wiley & Sons, 1992.

Cooney, Caroline. *Operation: Homefront.* New York: Bantam Books, 1992.

Dudley, William, and Stacey Tipp, eds. *Iraq.* San Diego, Cal.: Greenhaven, 1992.

Foster, Leila M. *The Story of the Persian Gulf War.* Chicago, Ill.: Children's Press, 1991.

Kent, Zachary. *The Persian Gulf War: "The Mother of All Battles."* Springfield, N.J.: Enslow, 1994.

King, John. *The Gulf War.* Morristown, N.J.: Silver Burdett Press, 1991.

Salzman, Marian. *War and Peace in the Persian Gulf: What Teenagers Want to Know.* Princeton, N.J.: Peterson's Guides, 1991.

Steins, Richard. *The Mideast After the Gulf War.* Brookfield, Conn.: Millbrook Press, 1994.

Videocassettes

The Aftermath of War With Iraq (29 min.), Oakland, Cal.: Video Project, ©1991. Information about the political and military results of the war in Iraq with footage taken during and after the war. Grades 7 and up.

Desert Storm, The Air Assault (60 min.), Plymouth, Minn.: Simitar Entertainment, ©1991. A look at some facets of the first month of Desert Storm air war. Grades 5–8.

Desert Storm, The War Begins (76 min.), Atlanta, Ga.: Turner Home Entertainment, ©1991. Events leading up to the fighting in Kuwait and Iraq from the summer of 1990 to January after bombing began in Desert Storm. Grades 7 and up.

Hell On Earth: The Kuwaiti Oil Fires (48 min.), New York: A&E Home Video: Marketed by New Video Group, ©1991. Grades 5–8.

Kids Ask About War (28 min.), Beverly Hills, Cal.: PBS Video; Distributed by Pacific Arts Video, ©1991. Questions children have about the conflict in Iran. Grades 5–8.

Sandstorm in the Gulf: Digging Out (30 min.), Oakland, Cal.: Video Project, ©1991. Analyzes the causes and possible results of the Persian Gulf War. Grades 7 and up.

Index